HISTORY OF INVENTIONS

Air Transportation

From Balloons to Superjets

Tracey Kelly

BROWN BEAR BOOKS

Published by Brown Bear Books Ltd
4877 N. Circulo Bujia
Tucson, AZ 85718
USA

and

Unit 1/D, Leroy House
436 Essex Rd
London N1 3QP
UK

ISBN 978-1-78121-452-7 (library bound)
ISBN 978-1-78121-468-8 (paperback)

Library of Congress Cataloging-in-Publication Data available on request

Text: Tracey Kelly
Designer: Supriya Sahai
Design Manager: Keith Davis
Picture Manager: Sophie Mortimer
Editorial Director: Lindsey Lowe
Children's Publisher: Anne O'Daly

Picture Credits
Front Cover: Shutterstock: Samuel Borges Photography.
Alamy: Chronicle, 8, dpa picture alliance, 11, The Print Collector, 10, State Archives of Florida/Florida Memory, 12; Brown Bear Books: 17; Dreamstime: Brett Critchley, 9; iStock: MediaProduction, 20; Library of Congres: 5b; Public Domain: 4, 5t; 6, Architectual Digest, 21, US Airforce, 18, 19; Shutterstock: Kletr, 15, Markus Schmal, 16, John Selway, 14, Brad Whitsitt, 7.
Brown Bear Books has made every attempt to contact the copyright holder.
If you have any information, please contact: licensing@brownbearbooks.co.uk

Manufactured in the United States of America
CPSIA compliance information: Batch#AG/5624

Websites
The website addresses in this book were valid at the time of going to press. However, it is possible that contents or addresses may change following publication of this book. No responsibility for any such changes can be accepted by the author or the publisher. Readers should be supervised when they access the Internet.

Contents

Taking Flight

People have always dreamed of flying. But they didn't always have airplanes! They tried different ways to get into the air. The ideas didn't all work!

Hot-Air Balloon
The first flying machine was a hot-air balloon. It was made by two brothers. It had a basket for two people. It flew for the first time in 1783.

Gliding High

People made gliders with flapping wings. They thought they would fly like birds. It didn't work. Finally, George Cayley invented a glider with a fixed wing. It flew in 1853!

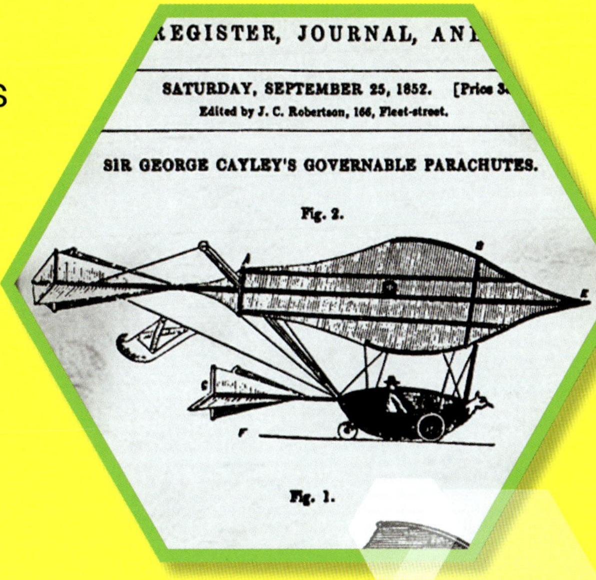

Hydrogen Balloon

Hydrogen gas is lighter than air. Balloons filled with hydrogen flew in the 1860s. Soldiers used them as spy planes in the Civil War.

Read on ... and find out how people made aircraft fly higher and faster.

Wright Flyer I

The Wright Flyer I was the first airplane. It was a biplane. Its first flight lasted just 12 seconds! It was invented by two brothers named Orville and Wilbur Wright.

Steering
The pilot lay on his stomach. He pulled wires. This steered the plane. Wooden propellers made the plane move.

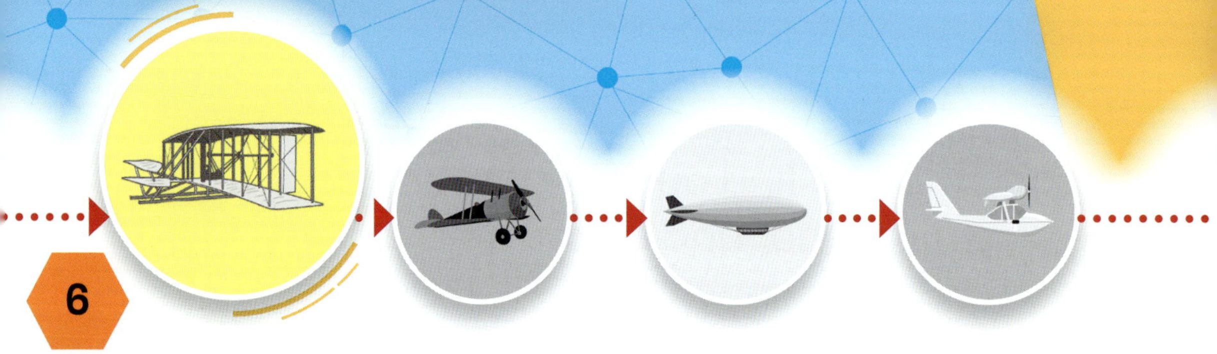

Wright Flyer I

The Wright Flyer I had a motor. Rudders moved the plane from side to side. Elevators moved the plane up and down.

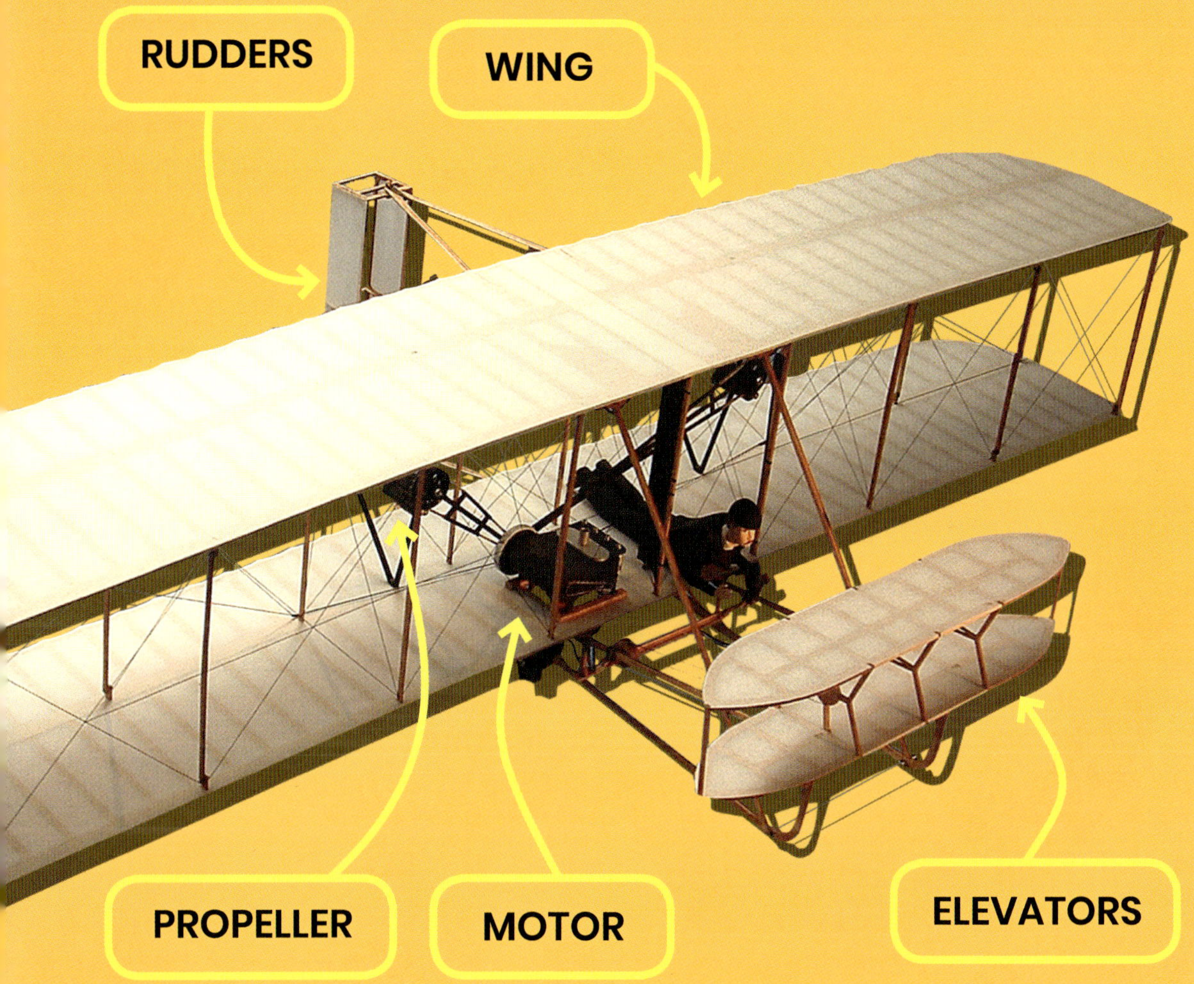

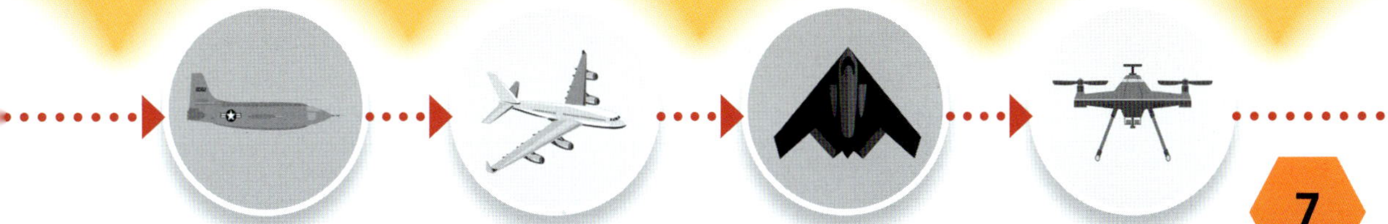

Dogfighter

Dogfighters were warplanes. They were very fast. First, they were used to spy on enemies. Later, they fought battles in the air. These battles were called dogfights.

World War I

The S.E.5 dogfighter fought during World War I. It had two guns and four bombs. It could fly at 138 miles (222 kilometers) per hour.

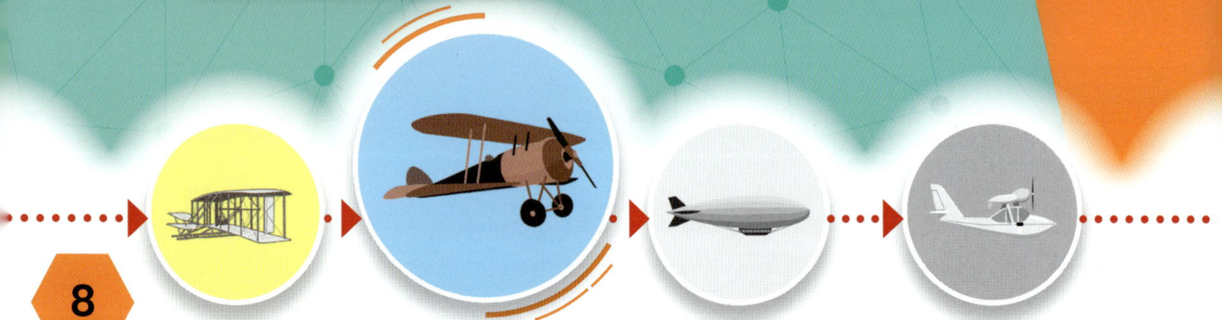

S.E.5 Dogfighter

This dogfighter was a biplane. It had a machine gun on top. The pilot sat in the cockpit.

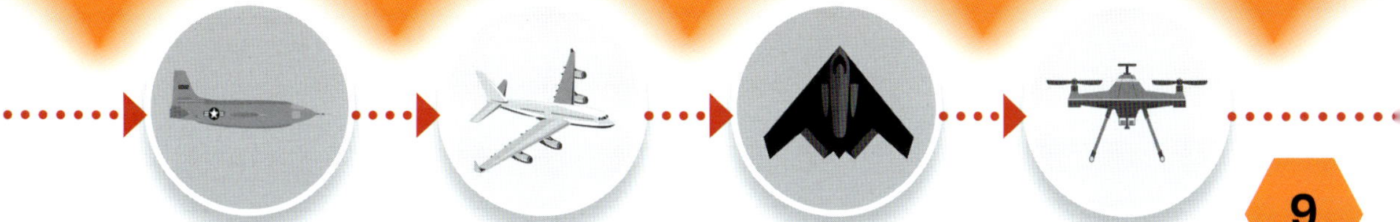

Airship

The airship was the first passenger aircraft. The passengers slept in cabins. The cabins were very comfortable. Airships could fly people thousands of miles. It took two and a half days to cross the Atlantic Ocean!

The Deck

The passenger deck had a lounge. It also had a dining room. Passengers could look outside through big windows.

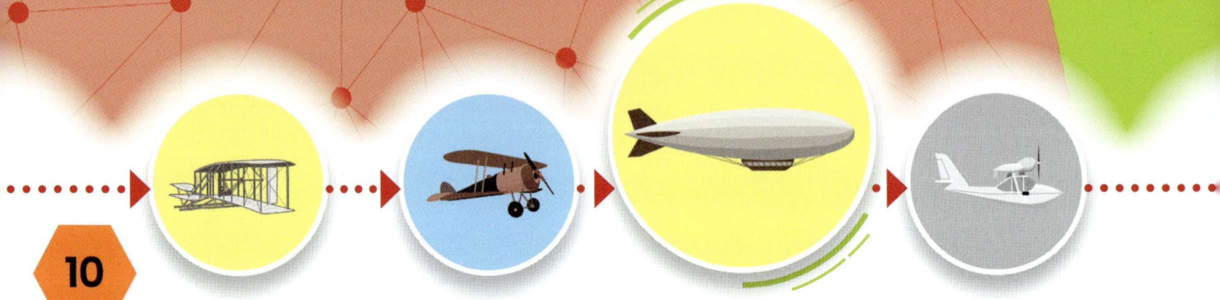

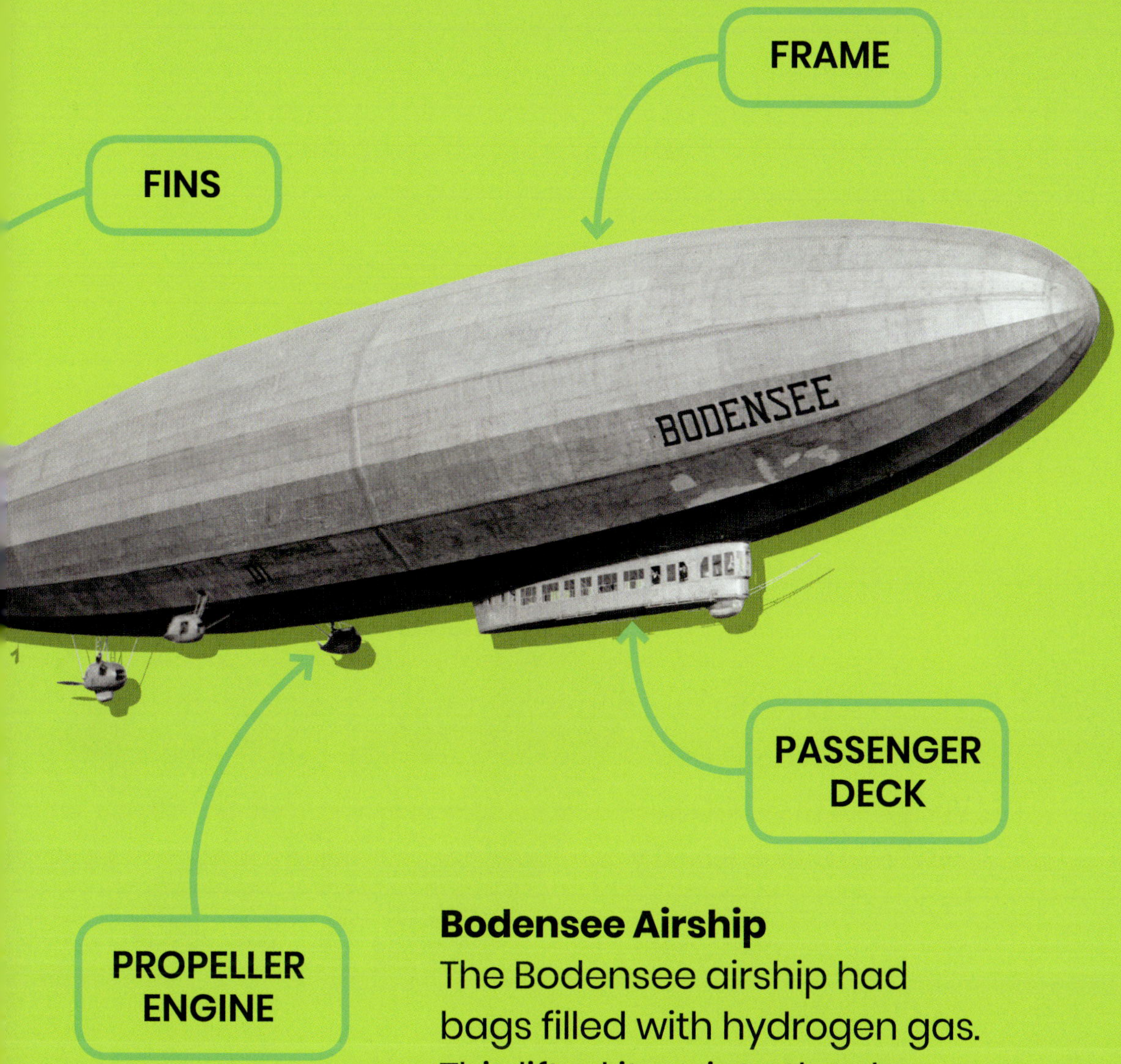

Bodensee Airship

The Bodensee airship had bags filled with hydrogen gas. This lifted it up into the sky. Propeller engines made it move. Fins helped it steer.

Flying Boat

A flying boat was a large seaplane. It could fly a long way. A seaplane could land on water. But the water had to be calm.

A-Listers

Flying boats were very comfortable. They were like luxury hotels inside. They were popular with celebrities and movie stars.

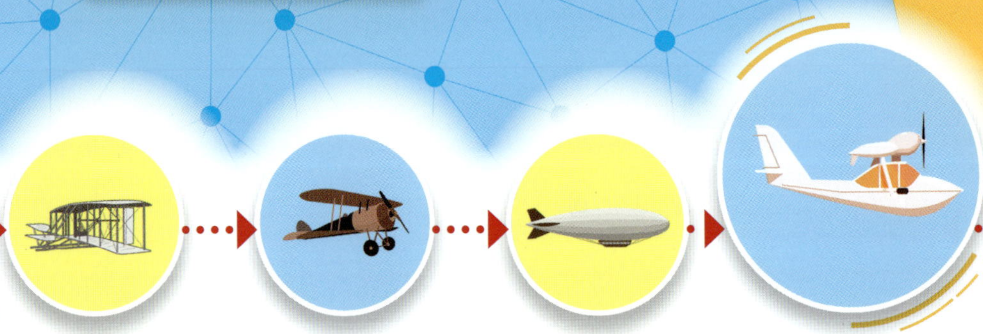

Flying Boat Hull

The plane's body was called the hull. It was shaped like a boat. There were floats under each wing. They kept the plane steady when it landed on water.

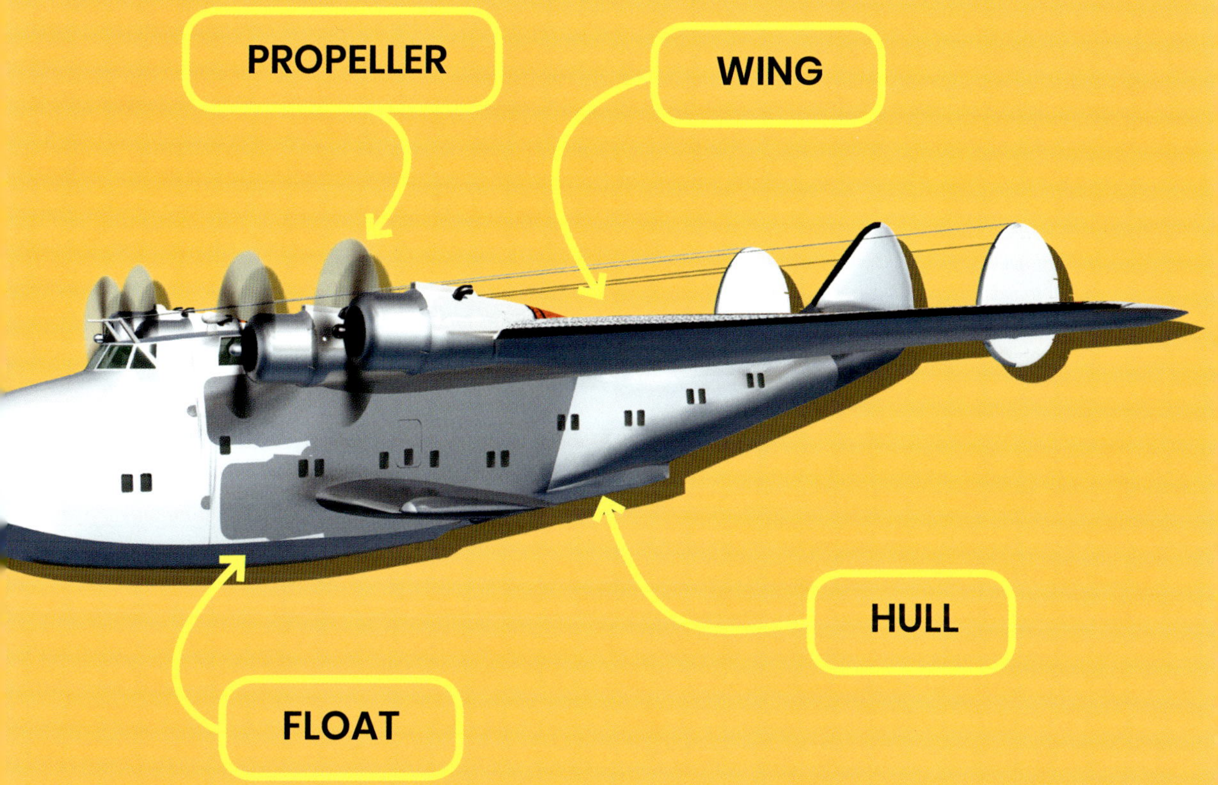

X-1 Plane

The X-1 was the first supersonic airplane. "Supersonic" means it flew faster than sound. It had a rocket engine for power.

Concorde

Concorde was a supersonic plane. It could fly from New York to Paris in just three and a half hours! A regular plane takes seven and a half hours.

X-1 Plane

The nose cone had a pointed shape. It could push through air fast. The X-1 did not take off. Another plane dropped it from the sky.

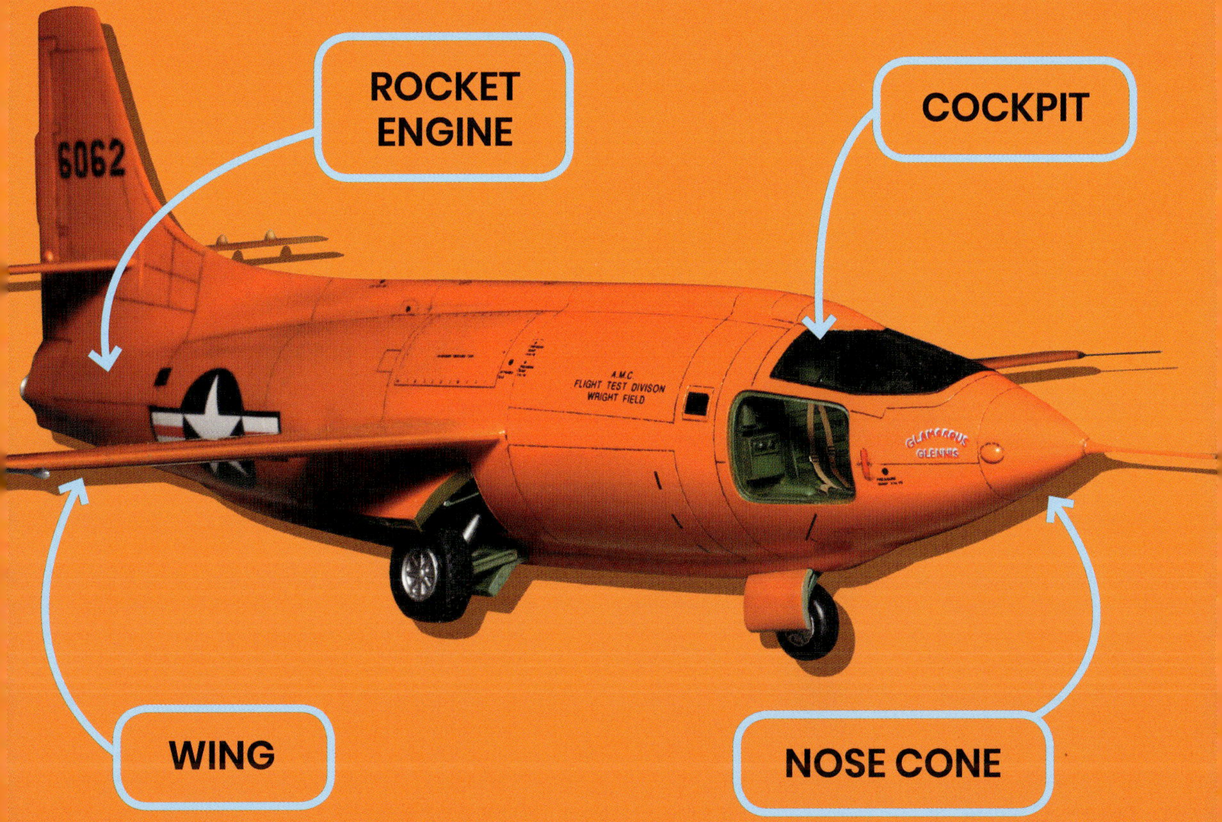

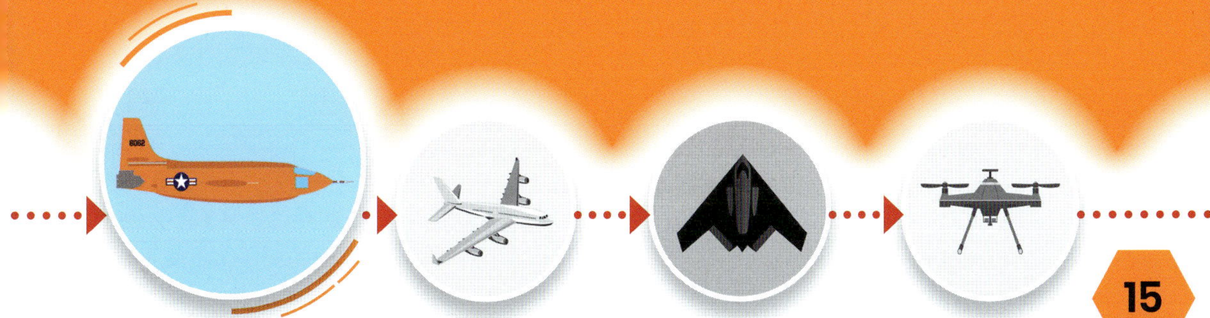

Jumbo Jet

The jumbo jet, or superjet, was a very large airplane. It carried lots of passengers. It made long journeys faster and more comfortable.

Boeing 747

The Boeing 747 was a famous jumbo jet. It first flew in 1970. The cabin had rows with 10 seats each. Passengers could watch movies during the flight.

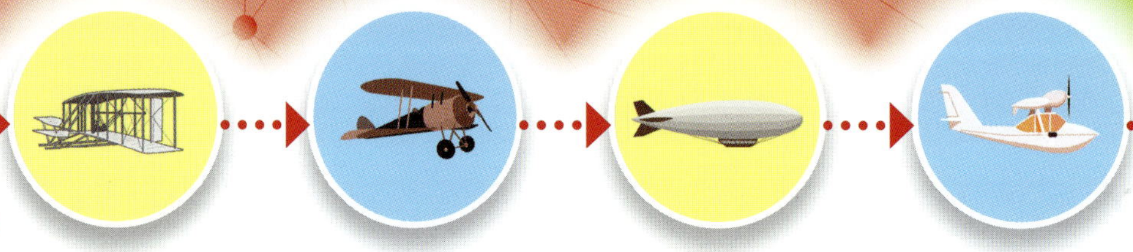

Superjet

Pilots sat in the flight deck. Cabin crew fixed food in the galley. A galley is a kitchen. There were four engines.

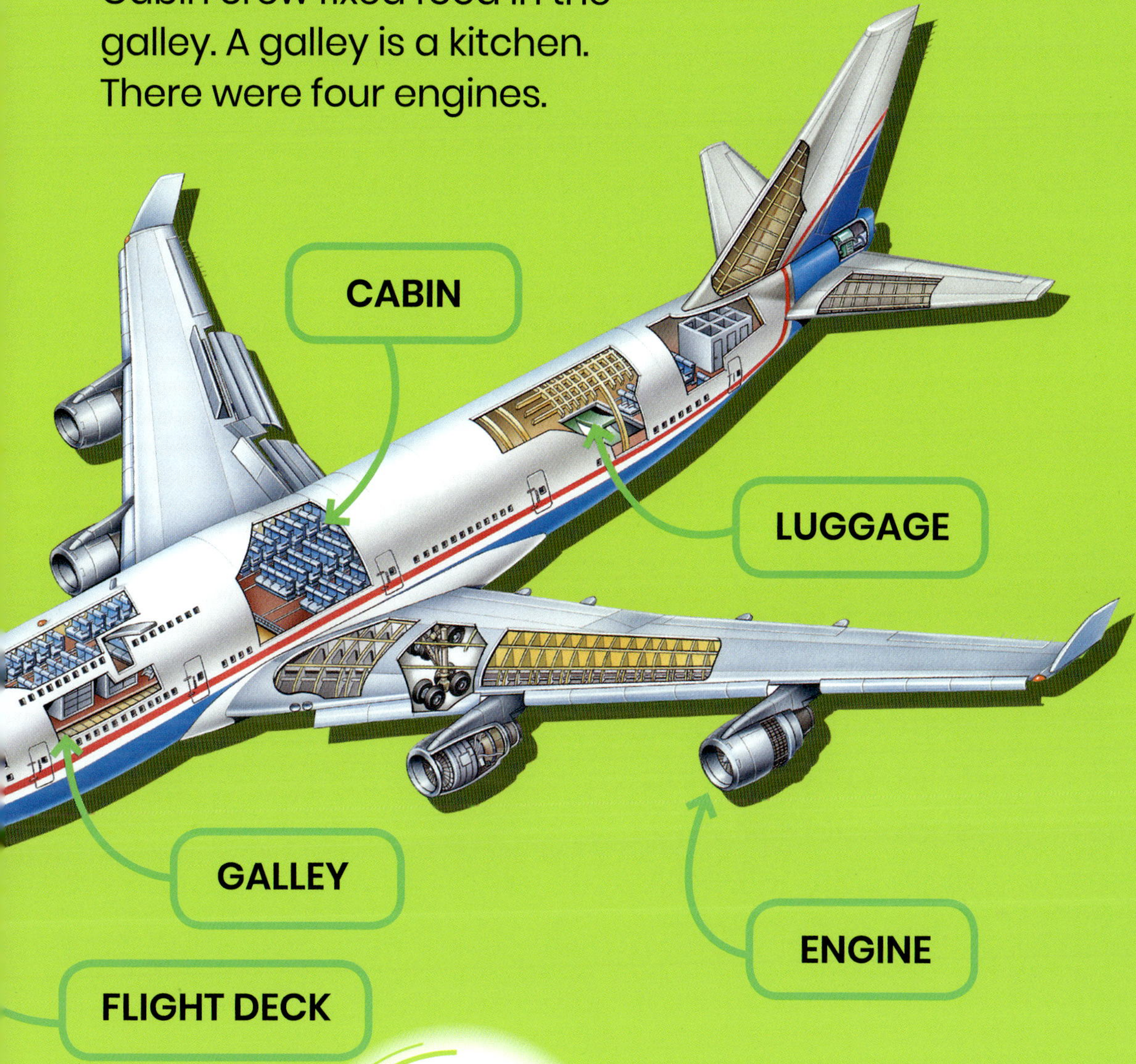

Stealth Plane

A stealth plane is invisible to radar. Radar sends out radio waves. The waves bounce off objects. People use radar to figure out where something is.

B-2 Spirit

The B-2 Spirit was a stealth bomber. It had a flying wing shape. It flew very high. This helped it stay out of sight.

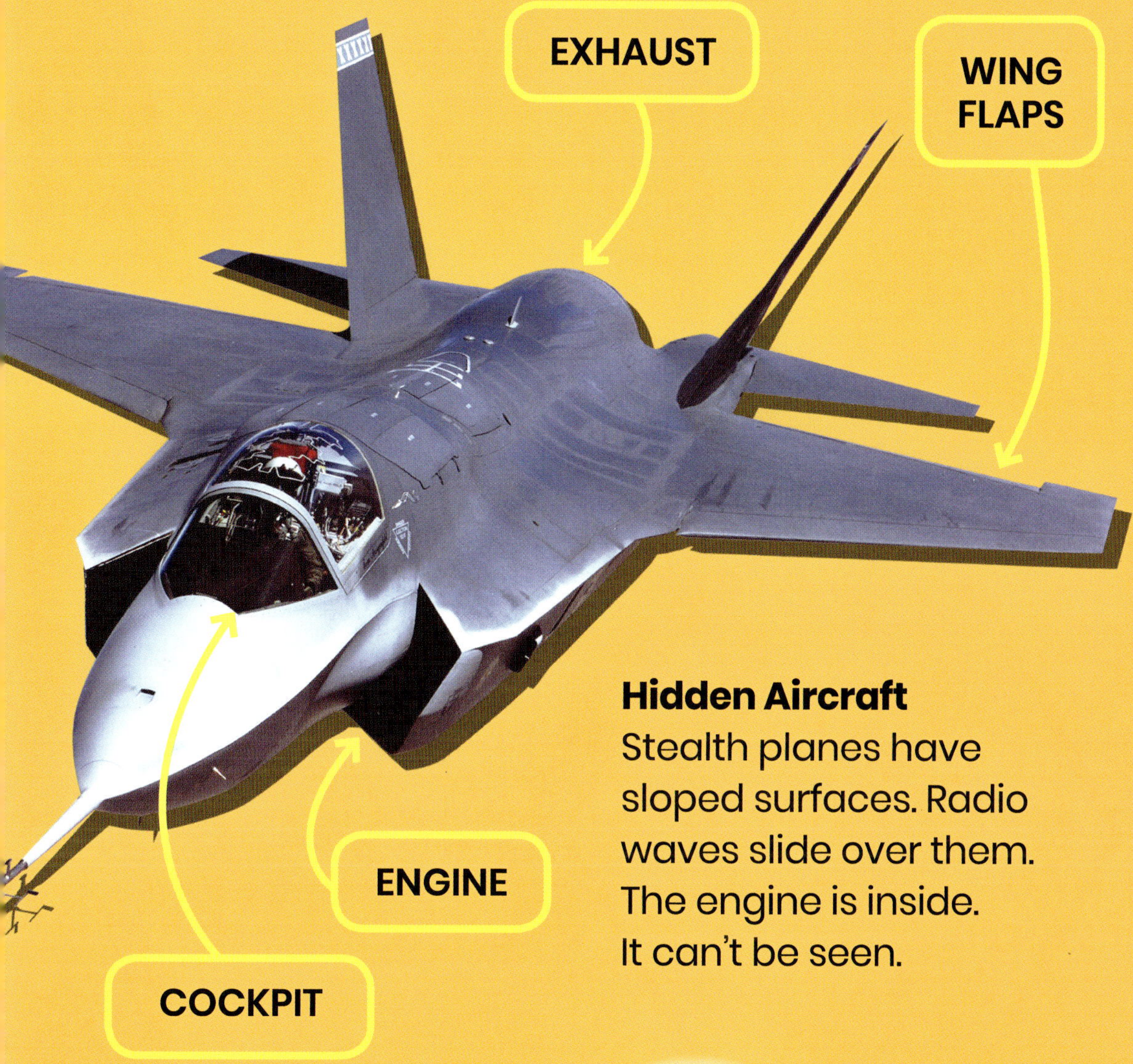

Hidden Aircraft

Stealth planes have sloped surfaces. Radio waves slide over them. The engine is inside. It can't be seen.

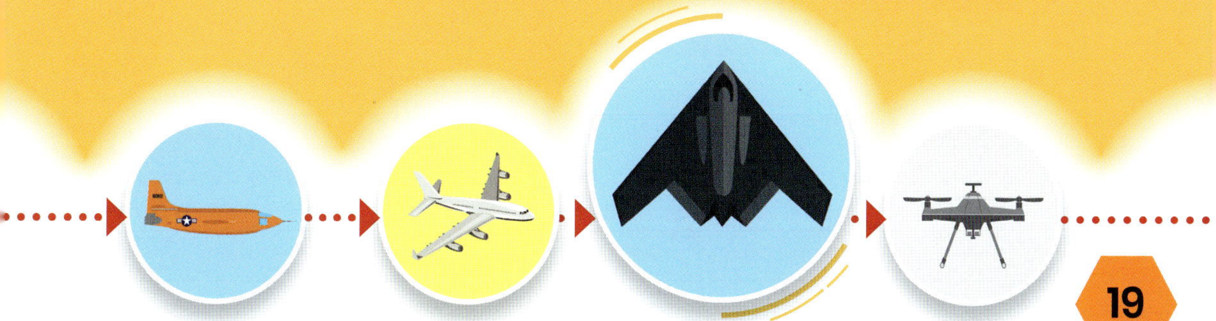

Future Aircraft

New aircraft are being invented now. Some will fly in space. Some will stay near the ground. What do you think aircraft will do next?

Delivery Drones

Drones are aircraft that fly without a pilot. People control them from a computer. Drones are already used for firefighting. Soon, drones may deliver pizza to your door!

Hypersonic Jet

Scientists are designing a superfast aircraft. The Antipode will fly from New York to London in 11 minutes! It may fly up to 16,000 miles (25,749 kilometers) per hour. Its wings will be fitted with rocket boosters.

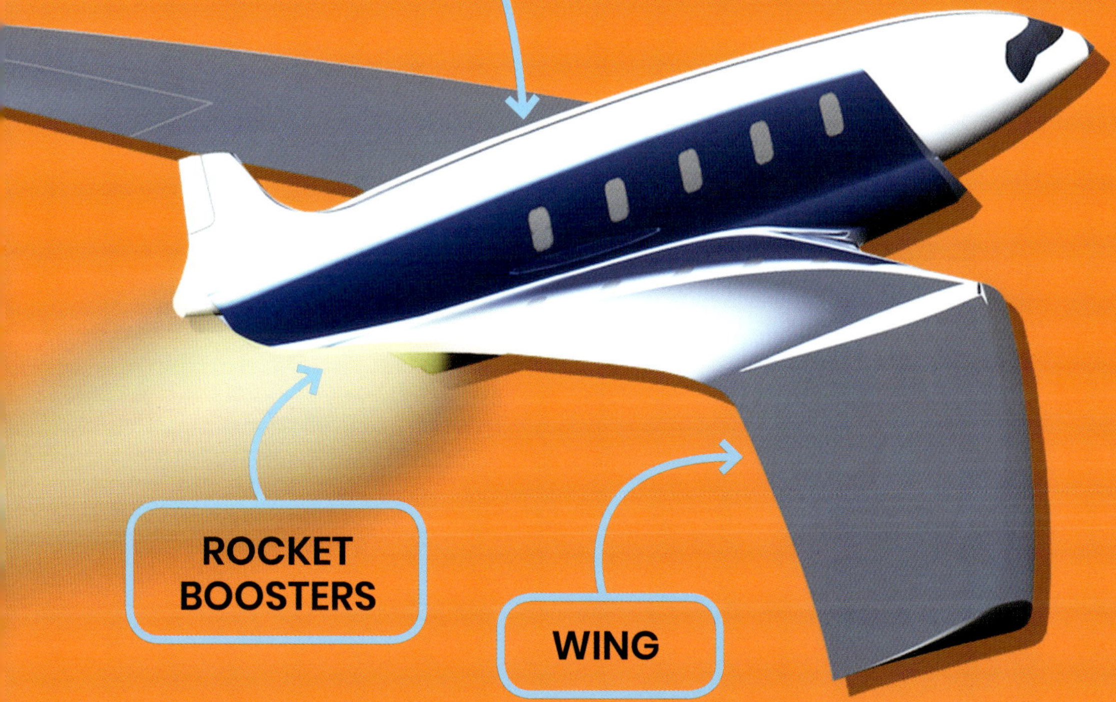

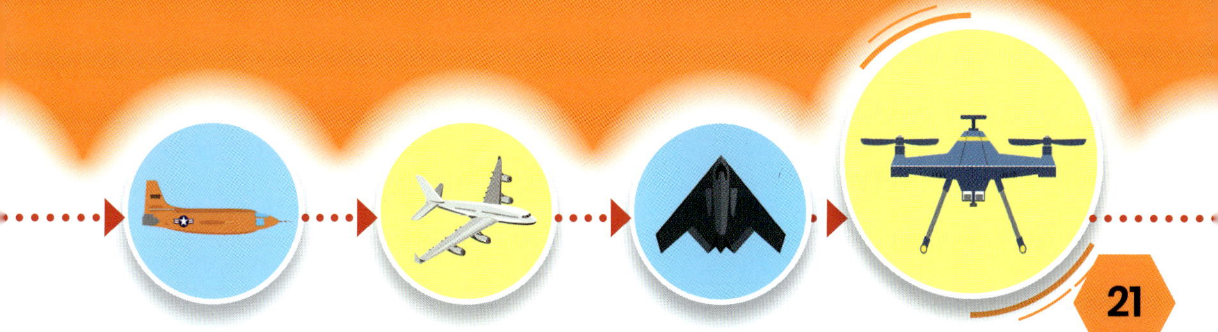

Timeline

1783	The first hot-air balloon flies over Paris.
1860s	Hydrogen balloons fly in the Civil War (1861–1865).
1900	The Zeppelin airship is tested.
1903	The Wright Flyer I plane flies for the first time.
1914–1918	World War I is fought in Europe.
1917	The Royal Aircraft Factory S.E.5 dogfighter is used in World War I.
1920s	Airships take passengers across the Atlantic Ocean.
1930s	Flying boats are used by wealthy people.
1940s	The X-1 plane flies faster than the speed of sound.
1969	Concorde flies for the first time.
1970	The first Boeing 747 jumbo jet takes off.
1989	The B-2 Spirit "stealth bomber" first flies.
2000s	Drones become common. They are used by the military and firefighters.
2010s	Hypersonic planes are designed. They travel superfast.

Glossary

airship A very large aircraft that has a body filled with hydrogen gas.

biplane An early airplane with two sets of wings. One is above the other.

dogfighter A combat plane that fights other planes in the air.

drone A small aircraft that flies in the air without a pilot.

flying boat A large seaplane that lands with its body in water.

hot-air balloon A big balloon filled with hot air that floats. It has a basket that people ride in.

hydrogen A gas that is lighter than air.

jumbo jet (superjet) A large airplane that carries hundreds of passengers.

radar A machine that uses radio waves to find something. Radar is used to find aircraft in the sky.

rocket fuel A fuel that explodes to launch an aircraft or rocket.

stealth plane A plane that cannot be seen by normal radar.

supersonic Flying faster than the speed of sound. Concorde was a supersonic plane.

Further Resources

Books

The Big Book of Airplanes
DK editors, DK Children's Books, 2016

The Wright Brothers (Great Scientists and Inventors) Emily James, Capstone Press, 2017

Websites

Find out about all kinds of aircraft and flying machines on this colorful site:
kids.kiddle.co/Aircraft

Discover how things fly, and do some cool experiments, on this amazing Smithsonian site:
howthingsfly.si.edu/activities

Index